How Wilby Got 20 Million...

Bill Belew, PhD, MFA

published by Do Good Books

How Wilby Got 20 Million

people to read his blog,

and How You Can Too

Bill Belew, PhD, MFA

For information or inquiries, write to:

Do Good Books
2134 Edgewood Dr.
Palo Alto, CA 94303

E-mail: wilby@dogoodbooks.com
Web: www.dogoodbooks.com

This book was designed using Adobe® InDesign® on Apple® Macintosh computers. The primary font is Calibri.

Interior design by Lewis Greer.
Cover design and illustrations by Benjamin Belew
www.mephistoape.com.

ISBN 978-0-9712723-7-8

Published by Do Good Books

10 9 8 7 6 5 4 3 2 1

Table of Contents

Introduction

A Blog by Any Other Name

The way I see it, the main problem with blogs is what they are called – blogs. What an ugly name. Blog also sounds too much like blah__g, blah__g, blah___. And unfortunately too many folks think that is what is going on at blogs: the blogger is just blah-blah-blahing away about their love life or lack of, their job or lack of, their rants and the like.

Not so. Not me.

When people ask me what I do for a living, I sometimes just for fun tell them I own a network of dynamic web sites with interactive capability. Dynamic because they are updated often, even multiple times daily; and interactive because readers can comment and give feedback to the author.

To which I get, "Ooo..." "Whoa!" or "Cool." And more often than not a blank stare and, "Huh!?"

To that last group I explain, "I own a blog network."

At which point they roll their eyes and think so loudly I can hear the thought bubble pop after they think, "The guy (me) has no love life, no job, and just gripes a lot online because he has nothing else to do."

Also not so.

I do have a love life (I don't write about that as it's really no one else's business), and a job, and I am definitely not a griper. Another more famous Will than I, Will Rogers, cured me of complaining with one his nuggets of wisdom. He said something like, "I used to complain about not having any shoes until one day I saw a man with no feet." I don't complain in my blogs or in real life, and I don't particularly care to read when others whine either. Besides, blogging can be a lot of good things, one of which is it can produce income.

This is a book about how to create a successful blog. Success, of course, is relative. Some bloggers might measure it by how many people showed up at their site today, yesterday, this month or this year. Some preachers I know (okay, all the preachers I know) rightly or wrongly measure success by how many people show up in church on Sundays. Others might determine success by the number of books they sell to visitors at their sites, while others will be happy about an increase in comments they get and the difference they are making in the lives of their readers. Finally, some will be happy to just be writing publicly or getting the word out on something they are very passionate about. One way I measure success with my blogs is that the income from them pays my sizable Silicon Valley mortgage.

In this book, my simple goal is to tell you, the reader, by the numbers, from my experience (as opposed to theory), what it takes to get 20 million visitors or more to your blog or, for those aiming a little lower and hoping for results a bit quicker a thousand or so visitors to their blogs each day. What you the reader/blogger does for those visitors once they show up – show them ads, teach them something, entertain them, convert them or just use the blog site as a very findable platform for anything else you have to offer – is, of course, up to the you.

After giving reasons (I feel like the apostle Paul, "let the reader understand") why I have the authority to teach you how to be successful with your blogs I will address six key points:

How to get a blog started

Why anyone would want to blog

What makes a good blogger

What makes a quality blog

How much effort it takes to build a successful blog

How long it takes to build a blog readership of thousands daily

Much of this book focuses on numbers 3 and 4 and.

At various points you will see – for example – or some similar expression. WARNING: I am likely to wander off into a personal anecdote or even tell a Bible story of some sort. I do not apologize for being a Christian. Applying Christian principles to the blogosphere has brought my blogs and me to where we are. And I do like to tell stories. So, feel free to skip the anecdotes, although they will help illustrate some key points and if nothing else let you know more about me.

It is my sincere desire that what you learn in this book, applied faithfully to your blogs, will indeed make a difference in your blogging life and in your life in general, not to mention in the lives of your readers. A reader, RWS, at one of my blogs, RWS, – "The Adventures of Wilby" – recently commented, "It's good to see that what you teach works."

If the principles here don't work for you, dinner is on me.

Chapter 1

Why Me Lord?

In 1971, Kris Kristofferson was 35 and I was in my senior year of high school. The third single on his fourth (same as the title to this chapter) album salvaged an otherwise mediocre collection of songs. I can remember singing along with KK in my '61 VW bug.

Thirty five years and change later and Kris is still singing that song. Me, I am humming the tune and wondering out loud, too, "Why me Lord, what have I ever done?" to be able to write a book on how to get readers to a blog site. I have an answer.

I made the leap to professional blogger early in 2006. I started with zero readers a day, no blog posts in the archives and no love. I can remember the first time someone showed up, the first comment, the first time someone yelled at me (yelling is more common than praise!), even the first time I got comment spam. Incidentally, "if you ain't getting comment spam you ain't nobody," are words to remember. In other words, if the spammers can't find your blog, neither can the search engines.

I was writing at a free blog host site and getting a share of the revenues, though it's relevant to remember there really isn't a smaller unit of money than the penny. It was tough going. But I met a guy through that network who told me he was writing for a business network, and he encouraged me to apply. I checked it out and soon learned they did not have anything in their netwok related to international business. (I had lived in Asia for nearly 20 years.) I proposed a topic and it was accepted. Www.panasianbiz. com was born. The blog was all about business in the Pan Asian region, and the network paid me by the post. Blog, blog, blog and more blogging, and little by little readers began to trickle in. I remember when I was excited to get 100 in a month! Then 100 in a day. We celebrated, bought ice cream, baked cookies...Then PAB gave birth to www.risingsunofnihon.com (all about Japan) and www.zhonghuarising.com (all about China). I proposed to the network oweners to write about the business of for-profit education. Accepted! Www.thebizofknowledge.com came into the blogosphere.

I had three sites going. We were given an upper limit on how much we could write and I hit the limit every month...every, every month. I wrote 15 posts of 200+ words each and every day...every, every day. (Praise God for schedulers so I didn't have to publish every day. The publishing tool did that for me.) Three of these sites grew to more than one million page views. The one that didn't was handed off to another writer. PAB is over 10 million views - about half of that is on China and the other half is on India.

There were some lean months during that time to be sure, not to mention when the blog network I was part of fell out of Google love and lost almost ALL of its traffic. Google accounts for about two-thirds of all traffic that a good site gets. Like 'em or love 'em, bloggers who try to make money with their sites work for Google. I could say, "I work for Google." But that topic is beyond the scope of this book.

In those four years my monthly average income has been enough to pay my sizable Silicon Valley mortgage. I had to save up from previous months at times and borrow from coming months at others, but we have a home in Sunnyvale about two miles from Yahoo, three from Google, and two-ish from Apple, among other tech giants. (You would think Google could just leak enough of its $4billion quarterly profits my way to buy me a house. Not happening.)

I have written more than 12,000 articles, all of them around 200 words each, sometimes more. Do the math. 2.4 million words at seven characters each and the space bar. I've hit my keyboard some 18-20 million times. I have received about one page view per word. (18.4 million as of Feb '10).

My sites get some 50,000 page views a day. I have had more than 100,000 come in day, several times. More than 10,000 people have come in less than an hour to see a post about Sachin Tendulkar, a cricket player. Quite intoxicating to be honest, not to mention addictive. It is easy (not right, but easy) for a blogger to find self-worth in how much traffic they get, or low self-esteem if they don't get very much. I have an Excel spread sheet of how many views my sites have had each and every day for the last 1200 and some odd days. At one point I was keeping a record by morning, afternoon, evening and night. Lots and lots of numbers. Lots of wasted time. But now I know how many readers I can get if I follow a few guidelines and post a certain number of posts over a certain length of time. I know from experience - call it empirical data - what it takes. And I will share that knowledge with you here.

I have taken eight different topics to more than one million page views: (page view is how many pages are viewed at my sites as opposed to how many visitors came. The latter is called unique visitors.)

The topics are: China, India, Japan, Environment, Christian, Bollywood, Cricket, News Headlines. Following are a few screen captures taken from some of my sitemeters to give the reader confidence to believe that what I am saying is indeed true.

Take a look at the "average per day" for page views on the combined view reading, and at the total page views on the reports from Japan (RisingSon of Nihon), Environment (Greenpacks.org), and Bollywood (FilmyFair).

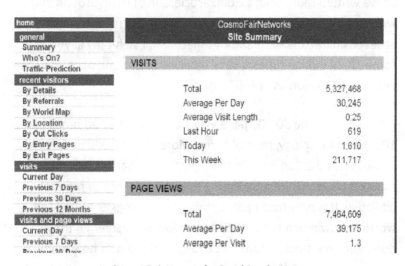

CosmoFairNetworks Combined Views

home
general
Summary
Who's On?
Traffic Prediction
recent visitors
By Details
By Referrals
By Search Words
By World Map
By Location
By Out Clicks
By Entry Pages
By Exit Pages
visits
Current Day
Previous 7 Days
Previous 30 Days
Previous 12 Months
visits and page views

RisingSunofNihon
Site Summary

VISITS

Total	1,673,780
Average Per Day	1,438
Average Visit Length	1:13
Last Hour	58
Today	144
This Week	10,067

PAGE VIEWS

Total	2,745,122
Average Per Day	2,096
Average Per Visit	1.5
Last Hour	105

Japan

home
general
Summary
Who's On?
Traffic Prediction
recent visitors
By Details
By Referrals
By World Map
By Location
By Out Clicks
By Entry Pages
By Exit Pages
visits
Current Day
Previous 7 Days
Previous 30 Days
Previous 12 Months
visits and page views
Current Day
Previous 7 Days
Previous 30 Days

Greenpacks.org
Site Summary

VISITS

Total	1,675,235
Average Per Day	2,239
Average Visit Length	1:03
Last Hour	116
Today	111
This Week	15,673

PAGE VIEWS

Total	2,153,606
Average Per Day	3,005
Average Per Visit	1.3

Environment

| home |
| general |

Summary
Who's On?
Traffic Prediction
recent visitors
By Details
By Referrals
By World Map
By Location
By Out Clicks
By Entry Pages
By Exit Pages
visits
Current Day
Previous 7 Days
Previous 30 Days
Previous 12 Months
visits and page views
Current Day

FilmyFair
Site Summary

VISITS

Total	1,081,361
Average Per Day	8,789
Average Visit Length	0:36
Last Hour	264
Today	916
This Week	61,521

PAGE VIEWS

Total	1,565,781
Average Per Day	11,324

Bollywood

A few of my sites have more than two million views and a couple have more than 4 million each. One site has surpassed 10 million views.

The network as a whole gets some 1.5 million page views monthly.

A writer friend of mine attended a recent workshop of mine. We met again in a weekly critique group, and she told me that she attended another similar workshop held by another guy here in the Valley.

"He said pretty much the same kind of stuff," she told me.

I looked the speaker up – Peter Muffleslopper (Not his real name). His site gets less than 50 visits a day, IF that many. Indeed, he may know how to get traffic to a web site, but he hasn't done it himself. Another friend of mine, Jackson (not his real name, either), knows how to rock climb, do origami, and quilt because he learned how in a book he had read. But he can't physically do those things. He just knows how.

I know how to get traffic and I have done it, and I am doing it.Please don't consider me prideful or boasting. That other Will I mentioned previously, Rogers, also said, – "If you can do it, it ain't bragging." I just want you to have confidence when you read what I write here. This book is not a theory how you might get results if you follow certain steps. It's a report on how results were acchieved by following certain steps, again, and again, and again and again and again and again, and again and again.

And for those who care, I did NOT dress "the King." That's important to me because yet another writer's critique group wouldn't let me participate because they thought I had some connection to Elvis. Bill Belew (same name, same spelling, but no relation to me) was the costume designer for the King. I don't even wish I were him. That Bill Belew is dead. I am very much alive... living life and living it to the full.

With no sense of false modesty, honest to goodness, I do not consider myself a good writer. I know some good writers. I am not one of them. I know how to write. I can spell and punctuate and deduct points from my students who can't. But I cannot write particularly well. I spent some 20 years in Far East Asia. I went days, weeks without speaking a word of English. Indeed, there's a big hole in my English writing and speaking ability. I can read but I don't have the confidence in my word usage nor do I have the facility with words to make sentences flow and ooze clarity and tickle ears and... see, I can't do it. What I can do is write stuff that gets read. I know how to do that. And that's what a blogger wants – people to come to their websites. People come to my web sites. And I can teach you how to do that, too.

In short – If I can do it, you can do it.

Test: Fill in the blank – If Wilby can do this and he doesn't write all that well, then _____ can do it, too!

Answer is below.

Answer to test question: "I"

Chapter 2

10 Things to Consider When Starting a Blog

I am convinced. I can write enough pages in this book to lose your interest. That's not what I want to do here. It is my sincere desire to tell you what you need to know to get a blog started and get it read, not everything there is to know. I don't know everything. I don't know a LOT of things. I just know what I know and what worked for me and what can work for you. I also know some things that aren't worth knowing for blogging success. What I mean to say, if I didn't write about it here, it's not all that important at this point.

Are there other ways to start a blog than what I'll tell you here?

Yup.

Are there other free blog platforms than I'll list here?

Yup.

Are there better hosts for your blogs than I know about?

Maybe. Please let me know.

I want to get you started. I don't you bogged down in not being able to decide how to start or which software to use or, or...

I am going to have to stop giving out my real email address at workshops. After one recent workshop, one lady wrote to me so many times I finally had to tell her – "That was your last question. No more, please. The right answer to most questions is to make a decision, then make that decision work. There is not always a best way to do things. But there is a worst way. The worst decision is making no decision = no start."

Here are 10 things to consider when starting a blog.

1. Do you go it alone?

By this I mean, do you choose a freebie blog (Put 'free blog' in a search engine box and you'll get choices. I'll give you my preference below) and start writing and hope for the best? Or is there another way? Going it alone is doable, but there are tremendous advantages to starting off as part of a network. Going it alone, you have to find others to link to and hope they find you, or follow up on the comment you left at their blog site, or answer the email you sent them, or respond to all the comments left at your blog and the emails people send you. Not impossible, but hard. The more a blog is linked to other blogs that are linked to other blogs, the more findable a blog is. This is extremely important and I will explain why later. The independent blogger must find people to link to and find other bloggers to link to them. This means less time for writing and more time for schmoozing is needed.

Do I become part of a network?

Yes. Repeat after me.Yes. Yes. The advantages far outweigh the disadvantages.

Here's a blog post from www.billbelew.com

--- begin post ---

5 reasons to write for a blog network instead of going it alone

I have been asked not a few times – "What are the reasons/benefits, or why would a blogger would want to be a part of a blog network as opposed to going it alone?"

Here are a few -

1. Blogging alongside folk who have 'been there done that' can save a LOT of time and energy for the individual blogger who otherwise would have to learn things all over again, to reinvent the wheel so to speak.

2. Which sounds better – I get a couple hundred/ thousand unique visitors a day/month or I am part of a blog network that gets 50,000-75,000 unique visitors/day or 1.5-2 million page views a month?

3. Being a part of a blog network gives the blogger instant visibility. No begging to be included in another blogroll... you will already be there.

4. Having a tech support team do all the 'fiddling' behind scenes frees the blogger up to do what they are supposed to do best – provide content.

5. Need someone to interview, guest blog? How about someone in the same network as you?

A better question I think is – why should a blog network want to include you?

What do you have to bring to other committed folk who want to provide something unique, add to the discussion at large?

---end post---

If you can find a network that will have you, join. I'll tell you how in a moment.

The biggest potential disadvantage to belonging to a network is that the content you create may belong to the owners of the network. Make sure you find out.

How?

Ask whoever welcomed you or is trying to sign you up to the network, "Does the content belong to me?"

Generally, if you are paid per post as I was in the beginning, the content will belong to the network owners. If you have a traffic based, revenue share (you get paid by how many people show up and a portion of how much money the site makes) the content belongs to you.

I wrote for a network in the beginning and was paid per post. I eventually had to buy my content back from that network in order to make the sites, domains and the content my own.

3. What's my name?
The name of your blog doesn't really matter that much. Of course, if you can get www.toyota.com or www.house.com and so on, by all means get them. Good luck with that. Many, most, if not all the good names are gone. Rather, build your own name. I own www.billbelew.com. I also own www.PanAsianBiz.com, RisingSunOfNihon.com. How often do you think either of those titles get searched? The domain name is not all that important unless you want one that is easy to tell people so they MIGHT remember how to find you. Good luck with that, too!

4. What's my tagline? My categories?
Taglines are far more important than your domain name for your blog.

What is the focus of your blog? In 10 words or less, what is your blog about? What words will people type in a search engine box that might bring them to you? This is important.

You can see my tagline at PanAsianBiz.

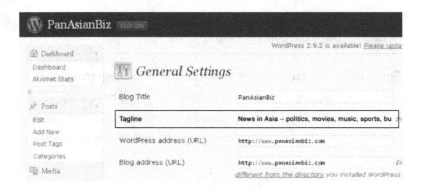

PanAsianBiz Dashboard

Tagline - News in Asia– politics, movies, music, sports, business.

What's the focus of your blog?

When a search engine comes crawling the little searchbots will be looking for the tagline. If the tagline of your blog is vague or ambiguous the search engines won't know if it wants to keep looking or not. Even if you say please. Search engines are dumb like that.

The next most important thing to decide is your categories. The focus of your blog ought to be divided into categories -10-15 at the most. The longer a blog lives the more likely you are to have too many categories. Not good! I know this, too, from experience.

Here's a look at the categories at PanAsianBiz:

PanAsianBiz Categories

I know, I know...too many! I am working on that.

The URL of a blog post will include the domain name, the category the post is in and the title of the post. Searchbots want these to be relevant to the tagline. Not only can searchbots be dumb, they can be persistent, too. The content of your post needs to be relevant to your title, category and tagline. No fair coming up with a great title on 5 ways to make $1,000 in an hour, then write about the second coming and how money won't be needed then anyway.

5. What software will I use?
As far as I am concerned, you have two choices: Blogger.com and Wordpress.com.

Choose Wordpress.com. Both are free. Blogger.com belongs to Google so you might think they get special treatment. Not so. As far as I know anyway. Wordpress is written for bloggers by bloggers. Wordpress has a lot of Word Camps that go on from time to time, and meetup groups where Wordpress nerds can get together and solve problems. I have used both Blogger and Wordpress and I don't use Blogger anymore. Sooner or later you are going to want your own site, have your own hosting, and it seems to me Wordpress can make that transition go more smoothly. GoDaddy, for example, has Wordpress ready to go in a few steps. Repeat after me – Wordpress.

6. Pick your look (template)

Flowers, oceans, cute, techie, funky. Wordpress gives you way too many choices. It's actually kind of fun to decide what your site will look like, IF you can make decisions. If choices overwhelm you, then ask a friend. Remember the worst decision is no decision. Choose one. You can make changes later if you like. You will find options at the dashboard where you login to WordPress. It's pretty intuitive, which means girls are better at it than guys as female intuition is generally sharper than male intuition, I think.

7. Where to put your sitemeter

Not having a sitemeter is like riding a bicycle without an odometer or driving a car without a gas gauge. Remember my '61 VW I wrote about previously? No gas gauge. Seriously. I just drove it till it ran out of gas, then flipped on the little 0.5-gallon reserve tank and hoped I could make it to a gas station... or too often push the Bug. Since then, I have not been without a meter to tell me how far I've gone or need to go. A sitemeter is free and available at www. sitemeter.com. It will tell you where people came from, what they searched to get to your site, how long they stayed, and how many pages they read on average while they were there. You can also learn a lot about your readers: their countries, time zones and other meaningless, um, useful facts. I could NOT have, still could NOT survive without my sitemeter. And if you belong to a network, chances are the tech folk will install it for you... for free. You can't beat that with a stick. Going it alone, you are on your own. And all the time you spend in the back end of your blog is not blogging. It's fiddling. You will feel like you are getting stuff done, but if you aren't putting up content, you aren't blogging. You're fiddling. I can teach you how to install a sitemeter, but that is beyond the scope of this book, too. I'll try not to say that too often.

8. Godaddy.com vs Blogger.com vs wordpress.com

Sooner or later the serious blogger will want to have paid hosting. Think sooner. Paying for something is like investing it in. And the more you invest in your blog, the more likely you will give the blog its due.

Vince Lombardi once said, "The harder a player tries, the harder it is to give up."

Indeed the more you put into your blog, the more likely you will see it through. It's the difference between riding a bike someone gives you and paying $1500 for a bike.

GoDaddy is not necessarily the best. But they are cheap, very blogger friendly and if you call the support number, real people answer the phone and stay on the line with you until the problems are solved. You don't see that too much these days.

9. wcbelew@gmail.com

That is my real email address. Email me and I will consider you for my network. I will not own your content. We will do some sort of revenue share ONLY if you make money and ONLY if your site is worth including. If you make nothing, you owe me nothing. Can't beat that with a stick either, if you ask me.

10. Blogging jobs –

Http://jobs.problogger.net/ is a real site and the owner of problogger.net is a real person, and a real nice person at that. The jobs are real and if you can pitch yourself and your blog idea, you can become part of one of those networks.

Http://www.examiner.com/Become_an_Examiner.html

4865 – secret number

The Examiner group is hiring and they pay well IF you can get readers. They help you get readers but not much. And they have a good support team but it's slow. The content belongs to you. Be sure to use my secret number. I have a bit of mojo with them as I have had more than 2 million visits to my Examiner sites (as of Feb '06). And if they hire you, I'll get $50. You and I can go out together to celebrate. I'll treat. Seriously.

Http://www.panasianbiz.com/submit-article/

This is my site. Let me know if you apply, so I can watch out for you.

Or search blogging jobs in Google or Yahoo or Bing, and wade through the results until you find something. Remember, if you're not writing, you're not getting read. Everything but writing is everything else. Putting up quality content is what matters most. Find a network, join if they'll have you and write.

Here is an exercise for you. After filling in the blanks, find five other bloggers or would-be bloggers to help you choose a name, a tagline, and five categories that will never go away.

Blog Exercise 1

What will I call my blog?

#1 _____

2 _____

3 _____

What's my tagline (focus)?

#1 _____

#2 _____

#3 _____

What are my categories?

1 _____

#2 _____

3 _____

#4 _____

5 _____

#6 _____

7 _____

#8 _____

9 _____

10 _____

Chapter 3

19 Reasons Why You Might WANT to Blog

It's funny (to me) that I am writing this chapter while watching the Super Bowl. Apparently the Super Bowl advertisers know (better than I) what I should be doing, drinking, wearing, reading, driving, putting under my arms, on my head, in my car, or on my face.

I do not for a moment think that everybody really SHOULD blog. But there are some folk who ought to give blogging serious consideration – writers (the kind that want to sell their books, build their platforms), speakers (the kind that want to motivate, sell, get their word or the WORD out), and others of that ilk. If you have something you want a lot of people to know about, then blogging is one way to do that, and a good way, at that.

In 2009, one of the head honchos (pronounced *hoen choh* if you want to say it right, not *hahn choh* as if that matters to most) of Technorati gave a presentation at Blog World Expo in Las Vegas. Technorati describes itself this way:

"... the leading blog search engine, Technorati.com indexes millions of blog posts in real time and surfaces them in seconds. The site has become the definitive source for the top stories, opinions, photos and videos emerging across news, entertainment, technology, lifestyle, sports, politics and business. Technorati.com tracks not only the authority and influence of blogs, but also the most comprehensive and current index of who and what is most popular in the Blogosphere."

They are right. Technorati is all those things, and the serious blogger will visit Technorati often.

The Blog World Expo is held annually in Las Vegas. The organizers say that BWE is "the first and only industry-wide tradeshow, conference, and media event dedicated to promoting the dynamic industry of new media including Blogging..." Tradeshow should be capitalized, underlined, italicized and hyperlinked. What else can you do to a word in print? Do that, too. For the most part, all the exhibitors at BWE are trying to sell the participant something. Leave your credit card at home. Still, there is stuff to learn at BWE and from Technorati.

At BWE's website you can learn these blog statistics:

1. Over 12 million American adults currently maintain a blog. What that means is that almost one in every ten Americans who go online do so to blog. Look around you. How many people can you count? ten or more? One of them has a blog. Is it you?

2. More than 147 million Americans use the Internet. That's almost half. Next time you go to church, remember all the people on one side of the church are online at some time or other.

3. Over 57 million Americans read blogs. At least two players in every basketball game or four in every football game, read blogs.

4. 1.7 million American adults list making money as one of the reasons they blog. I have made six figures (eight if you include beyond the decimal point!) blogging.

5. 89% of companies surveyed say they think blogs will be more important in the next five years. This only means something depending on the companies and how many were surveyed overall.

6. Pew Internet says 9% of internet users have maintain a blog. All those blogs. Something has to be good. Why not yours?

7. Pew Internet goes on to say that 6% of the entire US adult population has created a blog . And now we know why nobody answers the phone when we call.

8. According to Sifry, Technorati is currently tracking over 70 million blogs. See number six. Some of them have to be good.

9. Sifry adds that over 120 thousand blogs are created every day. This is not posts. This is sites. GoDaddy says zoom, zoom... as does Wordpress... and Blogger and...

10. There are over 1.4 million new blog posts every day according to Sifry. What in the world do all these people have to say?

11. 22 of the 100 most popular websites in the world are blogs . One of mine is #13,000ish. Just 12,900 spots to go!

12. According to Addage, 37% of blog readers began reading blogs

in 2005 or 2006 . It's not too late to get in the game.

13. 51% of blog readers shop online, says Clickz . What are you selling?

14. Clickz also instructs that blog readers average 23 hours online each week . See number seven. Find more info on these at http://www.blogworldexpo.com/

And here are five more very good reasons.

Technorati says of all bloggers, hobbyists and professional (that's me!) alike,

15. 63% of bloggers say, "blogging has led them to become more involved with the things they are passionate about." How much fun it can it be to write and share about something you have fun doing! Blogging allows me to do that. Blogging can be a great platform for you to do the same.

Professional bloggers say,

16. 71% of probloggers - "have a greater visibility in their industry." You got something to say? Need listeners?

17. 63% of probloggers say - "clients have purchased their products and services." What are you peddling?

18. 56% of probloggers say - "they are now regarded as a thought leader." Who is Mario Armando Lavandeira, Jr.? Mario's blog (gossip and garbage) is one of the top 100 most read sites on the net. Last year he was asked to be a judge for the Miss USA contest. Because of his pointed question to one contestant and his position on gay rights, that particular contestant lost. He also goes by Perez Hilton.

19. 40% of probloggers say, "they have been asked to speak at

conferences." I have been asked… and asked… and asked….
And quite often I have said yes, and thoroughly enjoyed it!

Still not convinced you should, ought, or might want to blog? Then never mind. You can stop reading now, because the rest of this book won't matter. But please pass this book along to someone who can benefit from it, and maybe they will thank you in their blog!

Chapter 4

20 Questions Every Wannabe Good Blogger Must Ask Themselves

Following this chapter there will be a test so, read carefully, please.

Here are 20 questions and answers that every wannabe good blogger must ask themselves.

1. Do I enjoy writing? If you don't enjoy writing, don't blog. Blogging is writing, too. It might not be novel writing, memoir writing or poetry, but it's still writing.

2. Do I have a message? I tell my online students that the reason most people can't write (can't speak, either) is because they don't have anything to say. Do you have something burning inside your bones? Jeremiah the prophet is one of my favorite characters. He preached gloom and doom for some 40 years.

(How fun can that be?) And not a few times he became discouraged. At one point he even decided to give up. But then, the passion for his message overtook him. When he decided he didn't want to preach any more, the overwhelming desire to continue became like a "fire in his bones," and he said he grew weary from holding it in. Passion will keep you motivated. But there is another motivator.

Here's a blog post I wrote about this:

--- begin post ---

Report: Blog workshop held on how to get more traffic and what you can do with it.

At one point during the workshop I touched on the 20 characteristics of a successful blogger.

On that list, near the top, was the word – Passion.

I jumped up and down, told the story of Jeremiah the

prophet and how he could not not preach because whenever he decided he wouldn't continue, the message of God burned like fire in his bones. See Jeremiah 20:9.

I was feeling pretty good about myself and that particular point until I read one of the comments in the feedback forms after the presentation.

"How do you get so passionate about cricket? or Bollywood?" I was asked. Thankfully, I didn't have to answer that on the spot.

It got me to thinking about what else might motivate a blogger.

The simple answer – hunger. Even a blogger has to eat, pay the rent, that sort of thing.

When I started blogging more than 4 years ago, I started it as a vocation. I decided I'd make a living at it or at least pay my mortgage (I do now!) no matter what.

Passion and hunger – two great motivators.

If you don't have a message burning inside you to get out, then make the commitment to live off your blogging come what may. Either one of those should keep you motivated.

If not hunger or passion – how do you stay motivated when there is nobody to tell you to write?

--- end post ---

3. Do I like to be the center of attention about my topic? A blog is a good way for folk to come find out what you have to say about your subject. That is you they want to hear and not

somebody else. Are you okay with that? Or do you prefer to be just another voice in a crowd? If so, a forum might be better for you.

4. Am I a self-starter? It is easy to start a blog. It takes character to keep it going. Nobody is likely to ever tell you, 'okay, better go post something now.' When I owned my company in Japan, I would hire teachers from overseas. Without exception, they were quite proud of themselves once they showed up in Japan. How hard is that? Get a visa, buy a ticket. Showing up is easy. It's what comes after that that matters.

5. Do I have self-discipline? Not only do you need to tell yourself to write, you also need to tell yourself to be consistent, to stay on topic and stay with it for the long haul till your voice catches on. Do you have the self-discipline that is needed to post quality stuff, the right amount of it, often enough, for the duration it takes to catch on?

6. Can I make the time commitment? You pretty much get what you pay for in blogging, too. You put in the time, put up the content and you will see a return for your effort. When I was in Japan, my students and I participated in yearly walk-a-thons. These consisted of 100km (62.1 miles) walks. We took pledges, then headed out. Generally speaking, there were two types of walkers. There were those who promised to go as far as they possibly could, to give their all, to walk until their feet hurt beyond imagination and they could go no more, at risk of being unable to work, mother or go to school the next day. Then there were the walkers who pondered out loud, "I wonder how long it will take?" The second bunch had made up their mind they were going to do it and it was just a matter of time.

Harry's neighbors could be seen sitting on the roof of their houses during a major flood. One shouted to the other, "Look at that hat in Harry's front yard!"

"Yeah, isn't it funny how it's going back and forth, back and forth in straight lines while it moves across the yard?"

"Nope, not really."

"Uh, why not?"

"Well, Harry told me yesterday that today, come hell or high water, he was going to mow his lawn."

7. Am I thick-skinned? Most people say they want feedback. That is until they start getting comments. What people are really saying is that they want people to blow smoke up their backside, to tell them they are doing a good job. They want comments so they can share with friends, "This is the reason I write!" Good comments do come but the majority of comments are not so flattering. Maybe I am just a bad writer or on the wrong side of my topic. That's possible. All feedback is good, but not all, not even most feedback is positive.

8. Do I enjoy being in the public spotlight? Once you hit publish, it's out there...in cyberspace...and folk can read it, quote you, blast you, praise you, report you and even forward your writing on to others. There is a delete/remove button in blogging, but 'takebacks' are almost as hard in the virtual world as they are in the real world.

9. Do I know my way around the back end of the store or in this case, the dashboard of my blog software? It is not necessary to know, but if you do, things can go a lot smoother... or not. Some folk think that when they are tweaking the look of their site, they are doing something. They think that when they are installing widgets or adding plug-ins they are doing something. They are. It's called fiddling. They are not writing, putting up content, getting read or blogging. The single most important thing a blogger can do is to put up content. Lots of it, regularly

over a long period of time. Everything else is everything else. Other things are important, but not as important as writing. That's why a blogger should consider being part of a network. More often than not, the tech support of the network will do all the necessary fiddling and the blogger can write. That is, the blogger can do what he or she does best and is most passionate about.

10. Do I have a sense of humor? Life is short, take it easy. Life is short, go gung-ho while the going's good. Be ready to laugh at yourself. Others will laugh at you and make fun of you as well. You might as well do it yourself.

11. Can I balance my ego with humility? There's a reason why Jesus said, "The meek will inherit the earth." And in another place, Solomon says, "Pride goes before a fall." Can you find the right balance? After all, it's just a blog.

12. Do I like to learn? Do you think blogging is ONLY about telling readers what you know, think or what you have learned? Can you still be taught? Or do you just teach? Continued learning keeps the blogger and his/her material fresh.

13. Do I enjoy reading? To be a good writer, reading is

fundamental. For example, reading other blogs enlightens the blogger as to what readers want to read. Reading a lot doesn't necessarily make a blogger a good writer. Writing a lot does that. Don't think just because you are surfing the web and reading a lot of stuff about your topic that you are blogging. That's reading. Blogging is putting fingers to keyboard and hitting publish at regular intervals. I'll say it again. Everything else is everything else or in a word, fiddling.

14. Am I an organized person? I can hear my wife laughing over my shoulder. I am not, but dang! I wish I were. Emails, comments, reading, writing, networking, handling multiple topics, feeds, going to meetups, chats... The other day I was in eight different time zones at once. I am on the west coast. I was chatting with my son back east and a fellow blogger in Romania. In another window, one of my writers in India and another in Indonesia were having a three-way chat about what time it would be GMT if a match was being played in South Africa. I think I was trying to make a point here but I don't remember now.

15. Am I a social person? I am not...but I wish I were. Then again, I have folk I work with in India, Pakistan, Bangladesh, Indonesia, Romania, Israel, Taiwan, Japan, China, the US and, and... Okay, well maybe I am a bit social... at least in the virtual world. If you need to press flesh... there is room for that. (Think blog expos and workshops about blogging... plug, plug.) But being comfortable and enjoying virtual relationships is a big plus.

16. Am I a creative person? A blogger doesn't have to be creative, but it helps. If you ask me, everything has to do with everything. I can even tie Michael Jackson to my Christian Worldview site if need be. Being able to relate your topic to what is going on in the real world, now, makes for a good, make that very good way to get readers to come visit your site and see what you have to say.

Here's an example of an article at Christian Worldview Examiner.

---begin post---

I know Carrie Prejean, but who in the world is Mario Armando Lavandeira, Jr.?

There are lots of people who know who Carrie Prejean is.

But who is Mario Armando Lavandeira, Jr?

Carrie Prejean is the good Christian girl who answered the question about what she thinks about gay marriage and why but might have lost the title of Miss America because of it. She opposes it, because that is the way she was brought up.

Mario Armando Lavandeira, Jr is nobody that anybody knows. And his opinion matters to nobody and he loses nothing for what he thinks.

Carrie Prejean has convictions and stands up for them at critical times.

Mario Armando Lavandeira, Jr is nobody, has no convictions and hides.

Carrie Prejean is identified for who she is.

Mario Armando Lavandeira, Jr steals for and exploits others.

Carrie Prejean is a role model at the young age of 21.

Nobody wants to be like Mario Armando Lavandeira, Jr.

Carrie Prejean has a future.

Mario Armando Lavandeira, Jr has no future. He no longer exists.

My hat's off to Carrie Prejean. She has my love and admiration.

Mario Armando Lavandeira, Jr gets nothing.

---end post---

17. Do I have perseverance? It takes time for a blog to catch on. The number one reason why businesses fail is because the business does not stay viable long enough for the idea to catch on. Imagine why blogs fail. The writer doesn't stick to it long enough. I will tell you from my experience how long (time), how often (pace), how much (quantity of posts) and what kind of quality (content) you must write to get folk to your site. Keep reading….

Here's an example of perservance.

Let me tell you a story about my older son (he drew the illustrations for this book).

When Benjamin was 7-years old, he and I participated in a biathlon (run-bike-run). We were required to run 5km (3.1miles), bike 60km (37.2 miles), and run another 5km. We ran the first 5km and he (7-years old, mind you) wasn't last. We took off on our bike. I was on my road racer and he was on his one speed BMX (big problem). We puttered along getting cheers and grins from all sorts of folk including the volunteers who were supposed to tell us when to turn.

"Go Benji! Isn't he cute?" (referring to me, of course… not!) cheered the girls.

But nobody told us when to turn (second big problem).

We continued on until we came to a big mountain. Anything uphill is big when you are on a one speed and are not old enough to have muscles. I realized we were not on the 60km course, but on the 100km course (62.1 miles) and we were climbing... um very slowly.

"Benji, we are on the wrong course. Let's turn around."

"No!"

Climb, climb, grunt...

"Benji, it's the wrong course. Let's go back."

"Uh, uh."

Grunt, grunt, climb.

"Benji, we can't climb this hill. It's too big. Besides it's the wrong course. Let's coast back down to the right course.

No answer. Two or three more turns of the pedal and he and his bike fell over.

"Now we can go back."

No answer...

Benji righted his bike, grabbed the handlebars and started pushing his bike up the hill!

I started crying. He started crying. And we both pushed till we crested the large mountain.

When we got to the top, Benji said, "Now, we can go back."

That's commitment, perservance, determination... all those good words... in a 7-year old. We finished the course and Benji now has his mind set on being an artist/pianist. He'll make it one way or the other.

What's your commitment level to your blog?

18. Am I me? Are you honest, transparent? If you are not being you, who will be you? A blog is your place. Be you and be the best you there is.

19. Am I willing to work hard? Blogging is not hard, it's not easy. It's kind of like learning a language. Wait, that's hard you say. Well, little kids can learn a language, right? Being a good blogger requires doing relatively easy things over and over again until it's done write, um, right. Putting up content is not that hard. It's the 'over and over' that's hard. It's dealing with the –sistent family (persistent, consistent, insistent) that's hard.

I have another son. Story time.

Micah, my second son, was a swimmer through elementary school, junior high and high school. At one time he and I were living in Buffalo, NY, and anybody who knows anything knows there is snow in Buffaloooo... especially in the winter time. He and I got up early one morning for a regular practice. I took him to practice in my little front-wheel- drive Toyota Corolla. No easy feat mind you, considering how much snow there was that winter. And it wasn't the first time either. Because of circumstances, Micah was swimming alone, in a 20-yard pool, with a private coach. His coach didn't show up... again! Micah was devastated, looked at me and said, "I quit."

"You can do as you please, you know. But remember you are not the only one who showed up this morning or every other morning for that matter. It's your call."

Micah went up to the locker room (he was 14-years old at the time) and I packed all the gear things up and waited.

Ten, then 20, 30 minutes went by. Far too long to change clothes. Then he came back out in his swimming suit, looked at the black board where I had written his work out and jumped in the water and started swimming. For two hours straight he swam, only glancing at the blackboard long enough to know what to do next. He swam, turned, swam, turned, glanced, swam, turned. Lots of turns in a short pool. When he was done with the entire work out, he jumped out and climbed the steps to the locker room, saying nothing. Ten minutes later he came out and we went home. Micah finished his college career on a full-ride swimming scholarship and is now a grad student in molecular exercise physiology at a University of California school. That's hard work and commitment. Do it or... there is nothing that comes after "or."

20. Do I know when to stop? This is hard for me. I am stupidly stubborn and at times just plain don't know when to quit. That's good and bad. If a person is stubborn and successful, it is said s/he has done well. If a person is stubborn and fails, they are just plain stubborn. Blogging often offers immediate returns. Publish something... people come. Publish more... more come. More... more... A blogger has to know when to turn off the machine, to go into the house, to spend time with family and other real people. If not, blogging can become addictive. I know. You might think that here is a dad who drove his sons mad. Not so. I never, ever, told my older son to practice the piano or the younger one to swim. Ask them. I had to tell them when to take a break. I wish I had been able to show them.

Time for a test.

When you are done, email me at wcbelew@gmail.com (Yes, my real email address) and let me know how you did.

Test – Exercise 2

Are you blogger material?

5 - You betcha!!!!
4 – Well, yeah, usually.
3 – Uh huh.
2 – Hmm, lemme think...
1 – Nope, not me.

Do I enjoy writing?	5	4	3	2	1
Do I have a message?	5	4	3	2	1

Do I like to be the center of attention about my topic?

	5	4	3	2	1
Am I a self-starter?	5	4	3	2	1
Do I have self-discipline?	5	4	3	2	1
Can I make a commitment?	5	4	3	2	1
Am I thick-skinned?	5	4	3	2	1
Do I enjoy being in the public spotlight?	5	4	3	2	1

Do I know my way around the back end of the store?

	5	4	3	2	1

Do I have a sense of humor?	5	4	3	2	1
Can I balance my ego with humility?	5	4	3	2	1
Do I like to learn?	5	4	3	2	1
Do I enjoy reading?	5	4	3	2	1
Am I an organized person?	5	4	3	2	1
Am I a social person?	5	4	3	2	1
Am I a creative person?	5	4	3	2	1
Do I have perseverance?	5	4	3	2	1
Am I me?	5	4	3	2	1
Am I willing to work hard?	5	4	3	2	1
Do I know when to stop?	5	4	3	2	1

MY TOTAL SCORE _____

100 – 81 – Show me the blog dashboard.

80 – 61 – Hold on while I get my coffee.

60 – 41 – I'll be there, I'll be there.

40 – 21 – Hang on. Lemme finish this program.

20 – I thought you said Bologna!

Test courtesy of InsideKnowMoreMedia
Scoring scale by Wilby

Chapter 5

21 Characteristics That Define Quality in a Blog

Quality is a subjective term. What is considered good quality to one person is not necessarily the same to another. One person might like a tune, and another may think "Huh? You call that music?" Quality in a blog can be defined, however. There are elements that, if included in a blog post, will increase the quality of that post. And the more a blog post has of these elements the better the quality. WARNING – there are a lot of lists, and lists within lists. Good luck!

Here are 21 characteristics that give quality to a blog.

1.   Original content
There's a reason this needs to be said. There are a lot of blogs that are spam blogs, spam news and the like. They are just repostings of someone else's orginal content elsewhere. Sometimes a blogger will write one post and put it up at many different sites. Please be

sure that the first site to get the original content will win out in the search engines in the long run. The blogger will want to write their own stuff. The blogger will want to not copy from someone else or let someone else steal their stuff. It happens a LOT.

2. 100 word minimum
This is a universal truth. For news sites to pick up a blog post and for advertisers to get a good feel for what ads to attach (if used) a post needs to be at least 100 words long. That's all? Yup. That's all. More is okay, too. My experience – 150-250 words works best. Anything longer than 300 words can be divided up into two posts and given part 1 and part 2 in the title. This is great to get readers to return. Blogs are one minute affairs. Readers don't study blog posts. They read them for information purposes or as discussion starters. There is a place, however, for longer and more involved posts. More on that later. And of course there are exceptions. See www.instapundit.com. He writes short and shorter and it works. But most cannot get away with that style. For me, the 150-250 rule has worked quite well.

3. At least one visual image
Find an image, a clip art or a photo to include in the post. There's an option to title the image and the title should be relevant to the blog post content. If you are writing about Michael Jackson going to church, title the photo/image – Michael Jackson goes to church or something similar.

Where to Find Free Images
Usually the first place I go to find free images is Google images search (http://images.google.com/). In some regards, I hate Google as much as the next guy, but they do good work. Google images provides a list of images from everywhere on the web. The blogger needs to be careful to ensure that any image he or she used from

Google images is not copyrighted (which should be obviously stated in conjunction with the original source of the image). If it's copyrighted, don't use it unless you get permission. This is done by contacting the photographer and asking. Same for Yahoo images search (images.search. yahoo.com/). Yahoo is useful, too. There are other sites, of course. Search free images. Try www.sxc.hu, www. imageafter.com, or www.morguefile.com. When using an image found via a search, it is good form to give a link back to the site from where it is found.

4. *At least one external link*

More often than not, a blogger might read another blog or a news item or some such source and want to comment on it or make a contribution to the discussion about the topic. It is good form, great form if it's another blogger, to give a link back to the source where you found your information. After all, if you started a discussion, wouldn't you want others to refer to you as the instigator? The answer to that question is, 'Yes.' Www.Technorati. com and blogsearch.google.com/ are great places to start to find other bloggers who may be writing about the same topic as yours. It's a great idea to say your piece and make reference, with link, to what someone else has said about your topic. After all, don't you like to be quoted? The answer is, 'Yes.' Here are a few more ideas – Ask.com, IceRocket.com, Blogpulse.com, Blogdigger, com, and Blogcatalog.com. I use Technorati and, well Technorati is the only one I have every used.

5. *At least one internal link*

An internal link is when you link to something else that you have written. I write about the evolution/creation discussion. Whenever I write something new about the topic, I link to something else I said about it, (e.g. in my previous post, 'The Evolution Carnival

Under the Boardwalk" (hyperlinked), I said, "Blah, blah...blog.") If people are interested in what they are reading they are quite likely to click through to the other post. This will increase your page views. Visitors are the number of people who come to your site. Views are how many pages they read. More page views means your site is good, relevant and interesting to the people who found it; that your site is worth reading, so much so they turned the pages to see what else you had to say and generally speaking, the more links you have pointing at your site from other sites, pointing to within your site, (that is you referring to your own posts), the better. It is especially good form to have backlinks from a variety of high-authority sites (See # 4). A backlink or trackback is when someone else has linked to your site in their article or post. When you link to others, they will link to you... sorta. People aren't as polite as they used to be. But that doesn't mean we can't be polite, does it? Search engine creators, (Google, Bing, Yahoo, etc.,) are always making their algorithms more complicated to thwart spammers. But links to and from a site are, and likely always will be, a critical part of the search engine ranking formulas. Links, internal and external, are essential for a blog. Besides, people are a curious lot for the most part and they will follow links you provide. The more links your blog has the better... to a point. You don't want a blog post that is nothing but links. But then there are sites that have nothing but links – Www.popurls.com is one and it gets a lot of traffic.

6. Two topic tags

Think! When you search for something, provided you use search engines, you usually use a one or two word phrase, right? And if that doesn't get you the results you want, you try some variation. This is what your topic tag is. Choose two words, sometimes three, or two or three two-word tags. Add these to your post via the dashboard. Some folks like to add a bunch of tags hoping that it will make their post more findable. This is called tag-spamming. It looks ugly and gets equally ugly results.

7. Has authority

See number four above. The more other blogs in the blogosphere that link to your blog the better. The more those blogs that link to your blog have blogs that link to them with lots of sites linking to them... yaaawwnn... the better. Suppose blogger A has 550 people that link to his site. And blogger B has 3 blogs that link to her site. Both write about the same topic as you. Technorati will tell you how many blogs there are that link to his, herw or your site. Which blog, A or B, will you hope notices your site and links to it? B... not! A, of course. The blogger will want to be sure that his or her blog is claimed by Technorati. Technorati has instructions for this, or your blog network tech support can do it for you. Incidentally, it should be further evident at this juncture why it is advantageous to belong to a blog network. There is instant link love if a blog network will have you. You get the power of links from other blogs in the network, and they from you. Of course, you are making out much better than the blog network.

8. Adds something unique

By virtue of the fact that I lived in Asia for nearly 20 years, I feel I have somewhat earned the privilege of commenting on many things Asian. Someone may be writing about family relationships in Japan. I do know something about that. I even know what does NOT work. The more your blog post can add that few others or even no other can add, the better the quality of that post. At some point a blogger would want to think that when topic A comes up, people will come to their blog to see what that have to say about the topic.

9. Is about something people want to know

There might be someone who wants to know who has the world

record for housing the most vacuum cleaners. That's not me. Chances are if you want to know a lot about a subject, there are other people who want to know as well. These days even niches are huge. I know of a guy that drives around the country doing tail gate parties at football games. He has a huge following, as in tens of thousands of readers daily. Make sure you are the go-to place on your topic.

10. Makes a contribution to the discussion

Not long ago there was a big earthquake on the backside of Japan. There were seven nuclear power plants that were shaken and threatened bakin' near the epicenter of that earthquake. I taught English to the engineers who built those nuclear power plants. I drove those streets weekly to teach my classes. When the world was thinking Japan was going to burn in a nuclear bucket, I had a different perspective because I KNEW the area firsthand. My blog about Japan was a great forum for me to add something to that discussion.

11. Has a great title

Clever titles aren't very clever. They are only cute if you have thousands of readers who are subscribed to your site and will get a link to your article via email or their news reader. But search engines don't do clever. Search engines want key word specific titles that directly corelate to the content of the blog. The first few lines will restate the key words of the title in some fashion to reinforce the title. At the end of this chapter is a pretty extensive list of good title patterns. Just insert the keywords that fit your topic. Lots of ideas –

Consider these 9 characteristics of a super blog post title:

The title

a. clearly states a benefit to the reader. The title promises to meet a specific need.

b. is descriptive. Simple is good, long is okay as well as long as the title can be connected to your tagline and is descriptive of the content

c. contains relevant keywords and phrases. A key word is what the article is about. Make sure there is a connection between the title and the content of your post, otherwise search engines and searchbots get confused (and confused rhymes with fused or fuses which blow.) You don't want to have a title about cricket streaming and write about the different shades of green balloons for birthday parties just to get hits.

d. makes a promise to the reader. The reader will get their wishes fulfilled, their dreams come true and life will be lived happily ever after... or not.

e. speaks directly but doesn't shout "BUY NOW!!!"

f. is honest. Sensational works, as does off-topic, but in the end your readers aren't likely to come back unless your blog titles are always filled with the double entendre. Come to think of it, I think that would make a great blog subject...a blog filled with titles that are all double entendre. Hmm...doubleentendre.net is available.

g. uses statistics and numbers. e.g. ,10 Ways to Lose Weight Fast.

h. mentions hot topics and famous people. Whenever possible, and it doesn't irritate the dickens out of your personal character, it works to relate a buzz topic or a celebrity to your topic.

i. appeals to emotional triggers - curiosity, fear, pain, pride or anger. e.g.,The 3 ____ That Will Make Your Co-Workers Envy You.

These nine tips were pilfered from an internal blog at a now defunct blog network where I used to write. Credit goes to KnowMoreMedia.

12. *Never runs out of ideas*

I have written more than 12,000 posts and I have yet to run out of things to write about. I have a friend who wrote a post - 111 Instant Blog Post Ideas. Insert that title into a search engine and you might still find it at BlogChalkTalk.

Here's another list of ideas: (Also 'borrowed' from the aforementioned internal blog.)

- "How-To" posts
- Tips, recommendations
- Your expert advice and opinions on any related topic
- Industry terms/definitions/vocabulary
- The history of your blog topic
- Current events
- Your opinion of a related webpage/blog with link
- Advantage/disadvantages
- Warnings, cautions, concerns
- Reviews/summaries of top providers/related companies
- Reviews/summaries of associations/governing bodies
- Reviews of top authors/journalists
- Product reviews (software, hardware, books, guides, service offerings, etc.)
- New product announcements/reviews
- Reviews/reports on conferences
- Upcoming conferences
- Training/training courses, both online and traditional
- Schools/Universities, degrees and classes

- Continuing education
- Certifications
- Careers/jobs
- Skills needed for success
- Contract/freelance opportunities
- Your own editorial/essay
- Interview with an industry expert and provide the transcript (Q & A style) over several posts
- "Link of the Week" (or "Link of the Day"): a link to a favorite webpage/blog
- Host a poll
- Run a contest
- Jokes
- Anecdotes
- Podcast interviews
- Vidcast interviews

13. Timely

There are any number of ways to find out what people are searching for or reading about on the web in real time. My two favorite are www.trends.google.com and www.alexa.com/hoturls. Of course, there are more - CNN has a list of top news, as does Google and Yahoo. Try Wikipedia Current Events. To predict what people might be interested in reading try the likes of http://www.nytimes.com/learning/general/onthisday/index.html

On such and such a date something happened and it will be remembered and/or celebrated. You can tell readers what you remember or what you think needs to be remembered or ask them what they remember. Where were they when Armstrong stepped on the moon, JFK was shot or Princess Di was killed? I remember where I was.

The University of North Carolina lists the seven basic news values as follows:

Impact: How many people's lives will be affected or influenced in some way by the subject of the story?

Timeliness: Stories that are more current generally have a higher value than those that do not. Journalists often compete for first publication bragging rights for timely stories and exclusives.

Prominence: Prominent public figures and/or officials also have a higher priority than a person who is relatively unknown.

Proximity: Local news almost always (emphasis on almost) has higher news value than something taking place far away.

Uniqueness: Odd news is definitely newsworthy...

Conflict: This one speaks for itself. War, civil strife, and other such occurrences are always newsworthy.

Currency: This may seem the same as timeliness but it is slightly different. Sometimes issues reappear in the spotlight and there may be some new element of the story worth covering. Think about the follow up to the death of a celebrity, the fall out because of a merger, that sort of thing.

14. Can attract repeat traffic
Consider thes tips on How to Get More Repeat Traffic

Watch for spikes - Check your sitemeter stats or what ever traffic tracker you are using at least once daily. I do it far too often, but I rarely miss a spike.

Welcome the spikers - If the spike is to your home page, quickly publish a new post that welcomes the readers coming from the source of the spike. I got surges from CollegeHumor for example. When I knew they were coming, I'd put in a note, "If you found this post/blog in today's College humor, welcome! Here's what this blog is about and why I hope you'll come back regularly or even sign up for an email subscription." If the spike is coming to a specific blog post, you can do the same by adding a welcome message at the top of the existing post or even at the bottom.

Show them where to go. At the end of all blog posts, consider adding a "Related Links" area where you share 3-5 articles they might also find interesting. There's a widget that can do this automatically.

Give them extra treats. Consider adding something extra to a spiked post - for example, turn a list of 10 tips into 15 or 20 or but put the extra information in a brand new post and ask visitors to click through for more on the topic. "Want more? Read on for part two."

Thank them for coming. You like to be appreciated. So do I. So do our readers. "Hang on! Before you go - I wanted to thank you for coming." Or words to that affect.

Ask them to come back. Did you think of this? Readers like to be invited to do things. Think about inviting them to subscribe to your feed or bookmark your site so they can return daily for the latest news and advice on your topic.

Promise more. Tell readers what you have coming up. Provide a tease. Say something like, "Liked this article? You'll love tomorrow's post. And don't miss next week's post series on a related topic."

Give readers what they want. If one post worked well, give your readers more of the same of the type of post that won their hearts in the first place.

Write for fanatics. Who do you want to attract to your blog? Write posts that attract diehards again and again.

Act quickly. Every minute counts when you get a flood of incoming traffic - the faster you take advantage of it, the better.

Prepare for future spikes. Why not prepare in advance a basic welcome message that you can tailor quickly for future spikes? That way, when a spike hits your blog, you are ready.

15. Engages the readers (solicits comments)
Following is a baker's dozen of ways to encourage people to make comments on your posts:

a. Ask. Do this at the end of your posts. "What do you think about ...?" or "Do you agree with ...?" or "Have you ever ...?" ... Ask questions that people can't help but want to answer.

b. Encourage people to talk about themselves. Has this ever happened to you? Where were you when...?

c. Make it clear that you welcome and respect all opinions. Let people feel like they are on equal footing with you. Your site allows and encourages differing opinions from your own.

d. Respond quickly to people's comments. Write a reply comment the same day, if possible - the same hour, if you can. And if there is an email address, you can write to your reader directly.

e. Make comments that encourage more conversation. When responding to a commenter ask a follow up question. Incidentally, this kind of give-and-take can work well in blog posts. I write a Christian site and I engage reguarly with a Jewish writer (on very friendly terms) and we are able to send readers to one another.

f. Pay close attention to the posts that get the most comments. Ask yourself if you should write more posts of the ilk that get comments or something else.

g. Leave your post open-ended. End with a question, for example. Or address one part of an issue and leave the other side untouched and ask readers to provide the other side.

h. Try to get people to think about what you've said. If you are not interested in your post, your readers won't be either.

i. Let people know that you appreciate their comments. Email a commenter and say thanks. I have on occasion elevated a comment to a post (giving credit) and followed up with my own opinion of the comments.

j. Ask Questions. Go beyond, "Do you agree?" by asking a question. "I think these are the top five cricket players. Who am I missing and why do you think so?"

k. Stir the pot. People love controversy.

l. Ping other bloggers. Ask another blogger that you respect to comment on something you have written. Who knows, maybe they'll think enough of it to make mention in one of their posts at their own blog site.

m. Leave comments at other blogs. When you leave a comment, you can most often leave a URL to your own site. It is good form when you leave a comment at another person's blogs for them to come do the same for you. People do NOT always follow good form, however.

Also, you might want to onsider these 5 reasons why blog comments can be good for your blog:

a. Commenters can become guest bloggers. It's happened for me not a few times.

b. Comments enhance the value and authority of your blog. Many people judge a blog in part by the number of comments it typically receives. I write about Creation. The evolutionists enjoy pounding on anything I say and even send their friends to come harass me as well.

c. Commenters help build relationships. I have virtual friends from all over the world that I met through my comments. I have stayed in the home of a person I met in my comments. My second trip to Blog World Expo in Las Vegas was free. The network paid for my entrance fee and the commenter put me up in his house. You can't beat that with a stick.

d. Lots of comments can increase traffic and backlinks. People love to refer others to a good conversation. See # 2 above.

e. Comments can generate ideas for future blog posts. Indeed I do get ideas for my articles from my commenters!

But by all means, watch out for trolls! After all that good stuff I just wrote about getting comments at your blogs, I also have to mention trolls. There are people who go about commenting on blogs just for the sake of picking a fight. And you can't tell who is serious and who is not. I have people at my sites that leave comments with names of household fixtures. As a rule, I don't engage with commenters who have not identified themselves. My time is better spent putting up content and encouraging discussion among the commenters even I do not engage.

16. *Pillar content*

Pillar traffic breaks the rules of 150-250 word posts. A pillar post is something that readers will come back to again and again, that others can't help but link to. I wrote a post – 21 must-know facts about India + map. I wrote it well over a year ago, yet it gets some 300-400 visits a day. That's a pillar post. I did 12 must-know facts about the Great Wall of China, 15 facts about Asia...and so on. Now if I could just write about 100 of those and get the same traffic for each, I'd be in business.

17. *Can go viral*

Viral = virus = bugs = everybody gets them at some time or another. A post that catches on is said to have gone viral. Following is a link to 37 viral post ideas - http://www.skelliewag.org/37-viral-post-ideas-you-can-use-today-103.htm.

A viral post is cool. Your site gets a lot of traffic in a short amount of time. But... all those visitors will leave and generally not come back. Now if you can get a pillar post to go viral, you might really have something. Especially if you can continue to follow it up. I wrote a post – 20 Hilarious Ratings of Professors at RateMyProfessors.com. It went viral. Some 30,000 people showed up. That was fun. But then where'd they go after that? Who knows?

18. *Encourages subscribers*

Here are 5 ways to get more people to subscribe to your posts AND to get subscribers to give you more blog traffic:

a. Ask. Ask your readers. If they liked this article please consider subscribing. Be genuine. But ask.

b. Anticipate. Tell them what they'll miss if they don't come back. Tell them what they can look forward and why they ought to subscribe now so they don't miss it.

c. Help. Put the button right in front of them. Make it easy for them to subscribe. Tell them how.

d. Thank. Say thanks to your subscribers regularly. Isn't it nice of them to subscribe to your content? Thank them and they're likely to stay.

e. Link. Link out to other blogs so they come running to see what you've got to offer. Link to your own old. Plus, email subscribers love clicking on links.

Here's a blog post I wrote about this a long time ago: (with a few minor changes to bring it up to date)

--- begin post ---

5 Reasons to Subscribe to My Blog

This is a shameless plug for this blog. A pitch. A plea. A petition.

I genuinely appreciate those who have taken the time to bookmark and/or subscribe to my blog. Thank you very much.

As for me, I can think of a few reasons why someone might want to subscribe, some reasons why regular subscribers would introduce this blog to a friend.

1. 11,343,711 and counting reasons. That's how many pages have been viewed at this blog. What's everybody looking at?

2. 5770 posts. That's how many posts I have written here at this site. There has to be something interesting in there somewhere. Point of interest - my best post here has received more than 100,000 page views. In fact, I

have two posts with more than 50,000 pvs and 20 with more than 10,000. Almost 200 of them have been viewed at least 1000 times each. What's everyone looking at? Ask me, and I'll gladly tell you.

3. 2370 RSS subscribers to date. Those subscribers have to have found something interesting to read. See number two. Maybe you will be interested, too.

4. I read through about 20-30 sites each morning looking for something that I think is interesting and relates to this blog, a lesson learned or something to put in my knowledge pack. Maybe you will be interested, too. Maybe you, the reader, will wonder why I would think the point is interesting.

5. I care about what I write, what I think. And, I hope that reflects in my posts. The things I write about, I do genuinely care about. What do you care about? Are we the same? Are we different? Why do you think so?

How do you subscribe to this blog?

It's easy.

Just click on the link Subscribe to Bill Belew.

Respond. Call me on the carpet. Make me do a better job. Ask me if it's the best I can come up with. Tell me if I did something wrong...or right.

But, consider subscribing. And invite a friend to do so also.

Do it today. Do it now.

Subscribe to BillBelew.

---- end post---

19. Has guests, interviews

So, how do you ask? A simple email, a phone call, a comment on their blog – those are common ways.

Following are seven keys to good guest blog recruiting:

- Introduce yourself and your blog.
- Extend the invitation to guest post on your blog.
- Identify a specific topic you would like for someone to guest blog about.
- Assure that you'll give clear author credit to the guest blogger, as well as a link to their blog/website.
- Give a timeframe for this guest post, but extend an open-ended invitation so they know you'd appreciate their guest posting at any time.
- Provide easy instructions for them to deliver the guest post content to you.
- Explain why you value or admire this person – the reason you're asking them to guest blog.

20. Is attractive to the social networks

Here are some social media sites you can submit your posts to: StumbleUpon.com, Del.icio.us, Digg.com, Newsvine.com, Fark. com, Reddit.com, Shoutwire.com, Lipstick.com, IndianPad.com.

I have received tens of thousands of visitors, views via this method.

My take on social networks is that they are indeed good for getting traffic. However, I did extensive study on this on my own. I recorded how much time I spent working the social networks, and submitting my stuff and getting it submitted and reading other's stuff and watching the increase in traffic. Indeed I saw an increase in traffic but it wasn't worth it in two regards. First, the people came, read and left and weren't likely to come back unless I worked the network some more. Second, the increase in traffic didn't relate to increase in income. I spent a lot of time to see more people come who didn't stick, click and in the end pay for my effort. It just isn't worth it to work the networks, if all you want is more traffic. A blogger is better off in the long run interacting with other like-minded bloggers at their blog sites, via comments and email or even in person, than to work the social media sites.

21. Has a long tail
One of the very best posts a blogger can write is a pillar post that goes viral over all the social media sites. If it is good, it will get linked to in a lot of places, making that particular post very findable in the search engines. Remember my 21 must-know facts about India + map. The initial spike that comes can be big. But the traffic that follows coming to that post over the long haul will be greater than the initial spike. That's the long tail. Every blogger hopes for a huge spike of a pillar post with a long tail. I have several thousand posts that have more than a thousand visits each. Not many of those posts got a thousand visits initially. They have just been around for a long time and keep getting found over and over again. That's the type of post a blogger wants to write.

Whew! I knew this chapter was going to be long and I did not disappoint myself. But after all, the heart of blogging is putting up good stuff, and these 21 elements define what is good, what is quality, what is the right stuff when it comes to blogs and blog posts. I'd like to say here that not a few ideas were gleaned from my involvement with KnowMoreMedia. Thanks goes to Dan, Easton and Kimberly for some of these points.

Now, get blogging!

Blog Workshop – Exercise 3

Choose from this list of blog title starters*, and use the lines to create your very own. (Hint: this list has endless possibilities!)

What do ___, ___ and ___ have in common?

_____

Can you pass this ___ Test?

_____

Top 10 Tips on ___

_____

Don't Buy the New ___ - Here's 5 Reasons Why

_____

How Oprah Does Her Laundry: Secrets Revealed

_____

Who Else Wants [blank]?

_____

The Secret of [blank]

_____

Here is a Method That is Helping [blank] to [blank]

_____

Little Known Ways to [blank]

_____

Get Rid of [problem] Once and For All

_____

Here's a Quick Way to [solve a problem]

_____

Now You Can Have [something desirable] [great circumstance]

_____

[Do something] like [world-class example]

_____

Have a [or] Build a [blank] You Can Be Proud Of

_____

What Everybody Ought to Know About [blank]

_____

Give Me [short time period] and I'll Give You [blank].

_____

If You Don't [blank] Now, You'll Hate Yourself Later.

_____

The Lazy [blank's] Way to [blank]

_____

Do You Recognize the [number] Early Warning Signs of [blank]

_____

See How Easily You Can [desirable result]

_____

You Don't Have to Be [something challenging] to be [desired result]

_____

Do You Make These [types of] Mistakes?

_____

How to [Mundane Task] That [Rewarding Benefit]

_____

How to ___

_____

How ___

_____

How I ___

_____

What You Should Know About ___

_____

Do You Recognize/Know ___?

_____

10 Ways to ___

_____

[Number] Types of [Category of People] — Which Group Are You In?

_____

Titles list courtesy of InsideKnowMoreMedia

Chapter 6

How Much and How Long?

It is in this last chapter that I feel I have something to offer the world of blogging that nobody else has or knows, or at least I have not seen any study such as the one I have done on the web or anywhere else in print. I have not read anybody else's thoughts on what I want to share here either. Indeed I, too, did not start out to learn the answers to the questions of how much and how long, when I started blogging. But I know the answers now.

The prophets of old often petitioned God when the people were Oppressed or when life seemed unfair. Jeremiah asked God, "How long will the wicked prosper?" He wanted to know how long the bad guys were going to have their way while the good guys suffered. John in the Book of Revelation asked God, "How long?" before God would be fair in His judgments.

One fellow might say he has been working very hard to find a job.

When asked how much effort he put into his job search, he might reply that he has sent out 20-25 resumes. Another fellow might say that he had sent out more than 600. That's how many resumes I sent out before I got a nibble on a job after moving to Silicon Valley right after the dot com bust. Bad timing.

How much work do I need to put into my blog? How long do I need to do it before I can see reasonable results? These are great questions. And for the most part the answers may escape us. Not me. I know the answers. I know what has worked for me.

At one stage in my blogging career, I was recording how many visitors I had at each of my blogs at various intervals throughout the day (3 hours apart and 6 times a day) so that I could predict what the traffic would be. Rightly or wrongly, I was placing value on myself and my blogs by how many people came. And for me, more was better. I knew at what pace I was writing, and I watched the traffic far too much. I knew or at least at the time thought I was wasting my time being so obsessed with the figures, but I couldn't not do it. Even now, I have an Excel spread sheet that goes across the page to GR or some other such two-letter designation. I have a LOT of data, by the day, for every one of my sites.

At one point a blog network that I belonged to fell out of love with Google, and the traffic stopped coming via Google's search engine results. I could pinpoint to the minute when that happened. I knew the numbers behind my sites and the network well enough to do so.

I knew after how many blog posts and at what pace (how many posts per day/week) about what kind of traffic I was getting, and in turn I also learned, after looking at the pattern of several sites, how much traffic I could predict would come if I worked at a certain pace. If I applied standards outlined in this book, over time I knew what to expect and pretty much when.

Following are screen shots of three sitemeters. The first is PanAsianBiz. The second is RisingSunOfNihon and the third is TheBizOfKnowledge.

PanAsianBiz was created first. In the 10th month, notice what happened to the traffic.

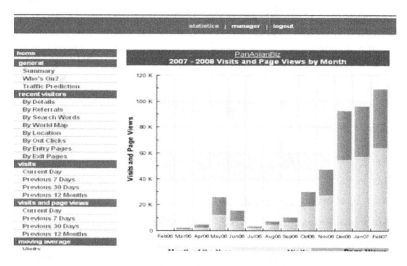

PanAsianBiz's 1st 10 months

RisingSunOfNihon was created second. Look what happened in the 7th month.

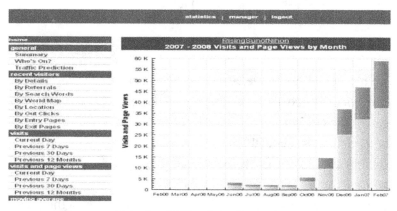

RisingSunOfNihon's 1st 7 months

TheBizOfKnowlege came third. Again, can you see what happened in the 6th month?

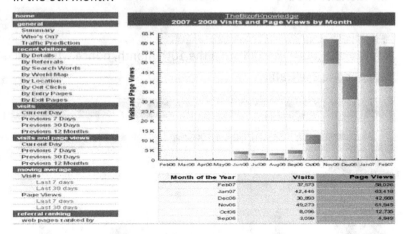

TheBizOfKnowledge's first 6 months

After 10 months, seven months and six months respectively, the traffic jumped. Leaped!? What happened? Why?

At each of the three sites, I wrote at a pace of five posts each day, every day. Every, every day. Thank God for schedulers! I wrote posts in advance and scheduled them to go out on weekends and other days so I could pry myself away from my dashboard. But not my sitemeters! I still checked them faithfully.

The simple conclusion to the how much and how long of blogging:

If a blogger will write the quality type posts explained previously, and work the networks, commenting and such as I explained earlier the blogger can expect their blogs to start growing organically after about 10 months. Organic means there is enough content and the site is vibrant enough that the search engines will notice it more readily and bring more traffic. A second blog will grow faster because it has the benefit of the first blog. A third blog might grow faster because I am smarter... in theory, of course.

My answers – a blogger should make it his/her goal to write five posts a day, every day for about 6-9 months (about 1000 posts total). After which that blogger can expect to see on average 1000-2000 visits a day at their site, if not more.

I have subsequently applied this strategy to other blogs, and sure enough the traffic came and it will work for you.

Conclusion

It's Not Easy, It's Not Hard

If a blogger wants to have several thousand visitors coming to their site daily, the plan is here. It's not easy, but it's not hard.

The hard part is doing the easy stuff over and over again till it catches on.

I have a pair of running shoes that have names. The left shoe is called 'Crush it.' The right shoe is called 'Bag it.' The names come from a story written by John Parker of "Once a Runner" fame. He tells about a time when he and some others were working at cleaning up the side of a highway. The trash was everywhere. For all intents and purposes, it was overwhelming. He picked up a garbage bag with one of those little trigger hands with a grabber on the end. Instead of thinking about the monumental task ahead of him, he just started crushing cans and picking them up one at a time and dropping them in his bag. Crush it, bag it, crush it bag it. One bag filled up, then another. Rinse and repeat. After a time, the highway shoulder was clean.

I have run 100 miles in a day in 23 hours and 40 minutes. Getting under 24 hours was the goal. That's a lot of running, and 100 miles is pretty far. But given the distance and a day's time I could complete it. When it got hard, I told my left shoe to crush it and my right shoe to bag it, and just kept at it until I was done – the 100 miles were finished.

Friends asked me what I thought about when I ran 100 miles. "Don't you get bored?" The answer is a resounding, 'Yes,' I got bored. What I thought about was, "Don't think." I just kept putting one foot in front of the other – crush it, bag it - until I was done. If I thought about it, the thoughts that came to mind were, "the distance is too far, I am too tired, I am too sore, I won't be able to work tomorrow", and so on." I could think of every reason in the world why I should have stopped. However, I preferred to not think. I told myself I would think about when I was done. I had made a commitment to complete the distance. That's all that mattered.

Blogging is not that hard. Make a commitment to putting up about 1000 posts within the next 6-9-12 months. Then put your head down and write. Write (crush it), publish (bag it). Rinse and repeat. And keep at it. Within a year you will have several thousand people coming to your site daily. The formula worked for me, again, and again, and again, and again, and again, and again, and again. It WILL work for you, too.

Please write to me a year from now and once you have reached your goal, and dinner will be on me.

For reference sake, my sites have since achieved these two milestones:

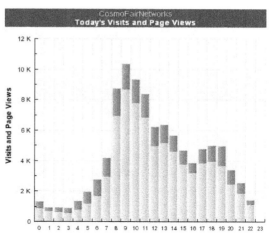

10,000+ views in one hour

100,000 views in one day

And yours can, too.

When they do, let me know. I look forward to hearing from you.

"Wilby"

www.ingramcontent.com/pod-product-compliance
Lightning Source LLC
Chambersburg PA
CBHW060941050326
40689CB00012B/2536